Kitchens, now and long ago

Sallie Purkis

This book is about British kitchens and how they have changed over the last hundred years.

You do not have to read this book from beginning to end. Just turn to the pages that interest you.

Contents

Kitchens nowadays

Kitchen un

Microwave oven

Electric kettle

Oven   Hob

Toaster

Fridge

Washing machine

Nowadays many people in Britain have a kitchen that looks something like this.

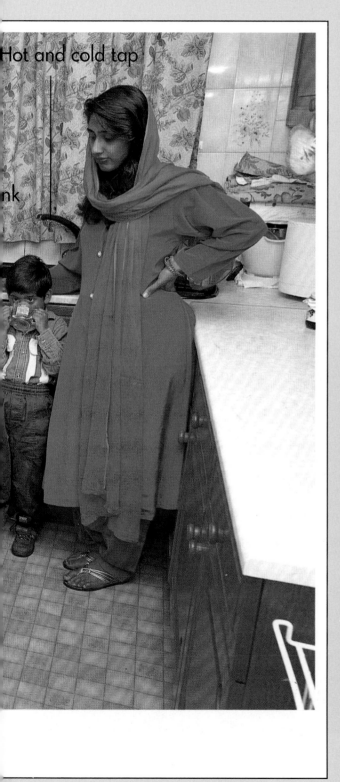

Hot and cold tap

nk

Many British kitchens today are fitted kitchens. There are no spaces between the cupboards, so it is easy to keep clean. There are lots of electric points, one for each kitchen machine. The washing machine even has its own set of taps at the back.

1990s

Cooking and washing up nowadays

The kitchen is where we cook our food.
Many families also eat in the kitchen.

⬆ Food cooks very quickly in the microwave oven.

Nowadays there are many different sorts of cooker to choose from. Some people have an electric cooker. Other people have a gas cooker.

⬆ Many modern kitchen sinks are made of stainless steel. This is easy to clean.

After the meal the plates, knives, forks, spoons and pans have to be washed up. Most people do this in the kitchen sink but some families have a dish washing machine.

Electricity nowadays

Most people have electricity in their kitchens.
Electricity makes the machines work.
It can also heat the water.

⬆ Food keeps fresh in the electric fridge.
The freezer is for storing frozen food.

⬆ You can even use electricity to make toasted sandwiches.

Most kitchens have a lot of electric sockets for the kettle, the iron, the fridge, the freezer and all the other kitchen machines.

1990s

Kitchen equipment nowadays

There are many other things we use in the kitchen like knives, scissors, graters and mixing spoons. Small things are kept in the kitchen drawer.

⬆ Some of the tools hang on the wall.

A lot of things in the kitchen are made from plastic which is light and easy to keep clean.

Some pans are covered with a plastic skin called Teflon.
They are called non-stick pans and are easy to wash
after cooking food in them.

↑ Non-stick pans come in many sizes.

Some dishes are made from a hard glass called Pyrex.
You can put them in the oven, in the fridge and in the
microwave.

Kitchens
fifty years ago

Many kitchens built fifty years ago did not have so many fitted cupboards as they do nowadays. Most kitchens had a china sink.

⬆ All the washing up had to be done in the sink.

Kitchens were not as easy to keep clean as they are today. The floors were covered in red tiles or in dark-coloured lino. They had to be scrubbed with soda and soap to keep them clean.

Scrubbing brush.

Soda.

SUNLIGHT SOAP
A LEVER PRODUCT
£1000 REWARD!

Dolphin BRAND
BLEACHING SODA and Water Softener 10.0Z 3D
For HOME LAUNDRY and GENERAL HOUSEHOLD PURPOSES

Kitchen soap.

⬆ A heavy bucket made of zinc was kept under the sink.

The sink was made of thick white china.
It had a wooden draining board.
Plates, cups and saucers broke if you dropped them in the sink.

Cooking
fifty years ago

Fifty years ago most people cooked on a gas stove. There were not many electric cookers.

⬆ The burners on a gas stove were lit with a match.

Most families chose to cook by gas rather than electricity. It was cheaper and they paid for it by pushing a coin into the gas meter.

⬆ Electric cookers looked like this fifty years ago.

Water to make tea was boiled in a kettle on the stove. Most kitchens had only one electric socket.

Kitchen equipment fifty years ago

Fifty years ago a lot of kitchen equipment was made of tin. The tin was covered with a white paint called enamel.

⬆ A bread bin, jug and mug made of white enamel.

Fifty years ago people had different equipment in the kitchen. They prepared foods like pies, jams and chutney using a wooden spoon, scales and a mixing bowl.

↑ Kitchen scales used weights in pounds and ounces.

↑ A Spong mincer.

In most kitchens the only machine was a Spong mincer. It had to be fixed to the table with a screw. It was used to cut up cold meat.

Kitchens
one hundred years ago

There was no electricity in the kitchen.
All the cooking was done on the kitchen
range which was built into the wall of
the kitchen. The range burnt coal.

◄◄ This painting shows what a
kitchen was like about one
hundred years ago.

The kitchen range
one hundred years ago

The range was made of iron.
The fire was kept alight all the time.
Every morning new coal was put on
and the old ash was taken away.

⬆ Every kitchen had a set of fire irons.

⬆ The children bathed in a tub in front of the fire.

There was an oven on one side of the fire. Some ranges had a boiler with a tap on the other side. Water got hot in the boiler and was used to fill a bath.

Cooking
one hundred years ago

Every day they cooked a soup or stew.
The meat and vegetables were put together
in a big saucepan and cooked slowly.

⬆ Water to make the tea was heated in a big iron kettle.

⬆ On baking day everybody wanted to be near the kitchen range.

Once a week there was a baking day when they made
bread and buns. They toasted bread using a long
toasting fork. Families who lived in the country kept a
side of bacon hanging in the kitchen.

Kitchen equipment one hundred years ago

A hundred years ago a lot of equipment in the kitchen was made of iron.
It was very heavy.

⬆ The handles on the saucepan got very hot when they were on the range.

The pans were very heavy and they were difficult to carry. It also took a long time to scrub the pans clean.

1890s

Glossary of words used in this book

China
China is made from clay with a white shiny covering called glaze.

Electric points
Electric points are the places on the wall where you can plug into the electric supply. They are sometimes called sockets.

Fire irons
Fire irons are tongs to lift coal onto a fire and a poker to poke the coal or wood into the flames.

Lino
Lino is short for Linoleum. It is a floor covering made from a mixture of oil and cork.

Pounds and ounces
Pounds and ounces are weights. They are often used today on market stalls.

Range
A range was an old fashioned cooking stove that was heated by a fire.

Scales
Scales are used for weighing things.

Sockets
Sockets are the places on the wall where you can plug into the electricity. They are also called electric points.

Stainless steel
Stainless steel is a silver coloured metal which is used to make sinks and saucepans.

Zinc
Zinc is a dull silver coloured metal. It is sometimes melted to cover things made of iron.

Index

a b c d e f g h i j k l m n o p q r s t u v w x y z
A B C D E F G H I J K L M N O P Q R S T U V W X Y Z